PRAISE FOR

THE GUYS

"The real achievement of Ms. Nelson's play is that . . . it gives credible and powerful voice to a very specific kind of pain that we crave these days to understand but from the outside seems only blindingly enormous and beyond sharing. . . . Perhaps the keenest message to emerge from *The Guys* is the assertion that writers—and actors—have a serious role to play in a grieving society."   —*The New York Times*

"The kind of quiet hybrid that the situation and the times— an era of a million pithy sound bites, booming rhetoric, and the numbing repetition of the CNN loop that followed the attacks—seemed to demand. . . . A small jewel of a play."
    —*Chicago Tribune*

"A generous, sad, touching play about the braveries of grief."
    —*New York Post*

"A courageous and riveting . . . play that tackles the horror of September 11 with an intimacy that's both unsettling and healing."   —*The Christian Science Monitor*

PHOTO: © JOYCE RAVID

ANNE NELSON was born at Fort Sill, Oklahoma, grew up in Lincoln, Nebraska, and graduated from Yale University. She is currently the director of the International Program at the Columbia Graduate School of Journalism in New York, where she also teaches international reporting. Her articles and photographs on the wars in Central America appeared in numerous publications in the United States and Canada. She continues to write and broadcast on international affairs, and lives in New York City with her husband, author George Black, and their two children, David and Julia.

THE
GUYS

THE
GUYS

A PLAY

Anne Nelson

RANDOM HOUSE TRADE PAPERBACKS

NEW YORK

A Random House Trade Paperback Original

Copyright © 2002 by Anne Nelson

All rights reserved under International and Pan-American Copyright
Conventions. Published in the United States by Random House, Inc., New York,
and simultaneously in Canada by Random House of Canada Limited, Toronto.

RANDOM HOUSE TRADE PAPERBACKS and colophon are
trademarks of Random House, Inc.

Library of Congress Cataloging-in-Publication Data
Nelson, Anne.
The guys / Anne Nelson.—1st ed.
p.   cm.
ISBN 0-8129-6729-1 (alk. paper)
1. September 11 Terrorist Attacks, 2001—Drama.   2. Funeral rites and
ceremonies—Drama.   3. Eulogies—Authorship—Drama.   4. New York (N.Y.)—
Drama.   5. Fire fighters—Drama.   6. Women editors—Drama.
7. Grief—Drama.   I. Title.
PS3614.E445 G89 2002
812'54—dc21   2002021311

Printed in the United States of America
Random House website address: www.atrandom.com
2 4 6 8 9 7 5 3

Photographs courtesy EGG the arts show
Thirteen/WNET New York
Photographer: C. G. Rubio

Book design by Victoria Wong

To the Captain, and to the guys.
And to all the captains, and to all the guys.

Landscape plotted and pieced—fold, fallow, and plough;
And áll trádes, their gear and tackle and trim.

All things counter, original, spare, strange;
Whatever is fickle, freckled (who knows how?)
With swift, slow; sweet, sour; adazzle, dim;
He fathers-forth whose beauty is past change:
Praise him.

—from "Pied Beauty"
Gerard Manley Hopkins

Preface

The Guys is based on a true experience.

I teach at the graduate school for journalism at Columbia University in New York, and I oversee some thirty international students. On the morning of September 11, 2001, we had sent them out, along with their American classmates, to cover the mayoral primary. It would be days before we knew that all of them had survived.

I had learned about the attack on the World Trade Center in a call from my father in Oklahoma. I watched the images on television until the second tower went down. Then, numb, I turned off the television, voted, and went to my office. I remember taking out my calendar and looking at it, wondering which of the events I had planned, if any, now had any meaning. I walked over to the hospital on the next block to donate blood. The emergency personnel turned me away. They were kind, but they wanted to keep the hospital clear for the wounded. They looked over my shoulder as they talked to me, searching the traffic lanes down Amsterdam Avenue for ambulances bearing victims of the attack—those ambulances that would in fact never arrive uptown. There were far fewer wounded than anyone expected. Most of the casualties were dead.

Twelve days after the attack, my husband and I took our children to visit my sister and brother-in-law in Brooklyn. Families in New York wanted to huddle, to eat together, and to talk quietly. A friend of my sister's called, looking for my brother-in-law, Burk Bilger, who is also a writer. The friend had met a fire captain and wanted to find someone who could help him. Burk was working on deadline, so I said I would help. The captain came over that afternoon. Once he got there, he told us his story: He had lost most of the men from his company who had responded to the alarm at the World Trade Center. The first service was only days away, and as the captain, he had to deliver the eulogy. But he couldn't find a way to write anything. Burk put aside his project and joined us. He and I reassured the captain and started to work. Together, the three of us spent hours producing eulogies. Burk and I worked in shifts, one of us interviewing the fire captain while the other wrote. It was clear to us that the captain, like many New Yorkers that month, was quite literally in a state of shock. Suddenly, a significant number of the people he was closest to simply weren't there. Yet in only a few days he was supposed to get up and speak before hundreds of mourners, to put something into words that would reflect their loss, as well as their esteem and affection for the fallen man.

Through the strange mathematics of chance, neither my brother-in-law nor I had lost anyone close to us in the catastrophe. But like most New Yorkers, we were stunned, grieved, uncomprehending. That afternoon turned into evening, and at last we finished the final eulogy for the services that had been scheduled. The captain thanked us, several times, and then said, "You should come to the firehouse and see what I'm talking about."

I did, a few days later. Like most civilians, I had never ventured beyond the firehouse doors. I saw the environment described in the play—the kitchen, the tool bench, the black boots set out on the floor ready for the firefighters to jump into at a call. I saw a long row of names written in chalk on a blackboard, which listed men as "missing" even though, since it was two weeks past 9/11, those men were surely lost.

The captain and I kept in touch. More services were scheduled. He came uptown, and together we wrote more eulogies. He delivered them at the services, and I would call to find out how they went. I could tell that every step was an ordeal for him, because he, utterly unreasonably, felt *responsible*. Like fire captains across the city, he wanted to take care of the families of the survivors, to compensate for their loss in a way no one possibly could. He would do everything for them he could remotely think of, and then berate himself for not doing enough. At the same time, he had to look after his men at the firehouse, whose world and whose way of life had been instantly and permanently changed.

The captain impressed me deeply. I thought that I had never met anyone so generous. I realized that generosity was the essence of the job—a firefighter's work was about saving lives, and the more often and effectively he did it, the happier he was. I also learned that like many of his counterparts, the captain had a boundless curiosity toward the world around him, including a fresh and eager appetite for the arts. That first meeting in September opened a door to the world of the firefighters, and as I continued to learn about them, my admiration grew. Over the coming weeks I read reams of press coverage on the aftermath of 9/11, but I felt as though my experience had given me a glimpse into another dimension. Three hundred and forty-three firemen lost is a number. I had had the privilege of being introduced to men—their qualities, their families, their daily life—in a way that made them real to me, and allowed me to mourn them and the others who had died.

In early October, some Argentine colleagues asked me to

appear on a panel in Buenos Aires. It was my first time out of the country since 9/11, and it made for a rough trip. The journey was a bizarre inversion of the time I had spent reporting from Latin America in the early 1980s. Now the airport that was filled with soldiers and submachine guns was in the United States—JFK. When I got to Argentina, I stopped at a corner bar for an *empanada,* and the waiter blithely informed me that "an anthrax bomb was just dropped on New York." He had gotten the story wrong, but it was a horrific half-hour before I found that out, a half-hour in which my only thought was that I should have been in New York with my children.

Over the next few days, I learned that the Argentines had their own perspective on the attack—or, rather, many different perspectives, ranging from the humane empathy of the many to the callous satisfaction of the few: There were some people, in some parts of the world, who saw the attack on the innocents of the World Trade Center as retribution for actions of the U.S. government. In the following days and weeks I learned, with the help of my international students, that each culture brought its own idiosyncratic interpretation to the event. Those interpretations made a jarring addition to my twenty-five years of experience in the fields of journalism, human rights, and international affairs. In my mind, the trip to Argentina came to illustrate the negative perception of Americans in other parts of the world, something Americans have difficulty understanding.

On October 18, shortly after I returned to New York, I attended a benefit dinner for my husband's organization, the Lawyers Committee for Human Rights. Sitting at my right hand was a pleasant-looking man named Jim Simpson, who was married to a Lawyers Committee board member, Sigourney Weaver. Jim and I were on duty as spouses, and over dinner, the conversation quickly turned to September 11. He told me that he had founded a small theater and repertory company in TriBeCa, just seven blocks from the World Trade Center. The Flea Theater had been flourishing but was now in danger of going under. Because of the attack, the area had been closed off for weeks, and once it became accessible, audiences avoided it because of the smoke and debris, as well as the general pall of disaster. Businesses all over the neighborhood were dying. The Flea Theater continued to operate, but the company was playing to empty houses. One of his young actors, Jim said, wanted to do a play that spoke to the situation directly. But what could that play be?

"*Antigone*?" I suggested. Maybe not. What about Brecht? We talked through the classical repertory, but Jim concluded, "It has to be something new. But it doesn't exist."

I commiserated. At the same time, I felt paralyzed as a writer. New York was full of journalists, and they were producing miles of newsprint. I was teaching and did not have a regular outlet. Yet writing was what I did—writing was how I had always made sense of the world. I felt a building pressure to write something to help me make sense of what had happened, and was happening now. Jim and I agreed that it would be good to have a further conversation, but I didn't really expect anything to come of it. But Jim followed up the next day with an e-mail. Somewhere along the way, I brought up the eulogies and told him how writing them had affected me. Jim encouraged me to write a play based on the experience. He suggested a "two-hander"—a play with two characters—alternating monologues and dialogue, a play that would compress the experiences and emotions of those first raw weeks into a single ninety-minute encounter.

I hadn't written a play before, but I was motivated to capture what I had observed and experienced through my conversations with the captain. I also wanted to try to help the theater. I loved the sound of what Jim had described—a small, noncommercial space, unpretentious but beautifully designed, with a young repertory company whose members were there for the love of the craft. It was the sort of enterprise that had drawn me to New York in the first place, and part of me felt— not entirely coherently—that if we could somehow keep it alive, it would deprive the attackers of another victory.

That night I visited the firehouse again. "Look," I told the captain. "I've been asked about writing a play. I'd like to try it, but I won't if you have a problem with it. And I won't include anything that you think would hurt anyone."

He considered it, and looked straight at me. "Do it," he said. As it happens, the captain is an off-off-Broadway theater buff. In keeping with his nature, he was worried about small theaters suffering from the attack and about the young actors who would be thrown out of work. And I think that he was clear from the very beginning that this might serve as a memorial of words, both to those who had died and to those who were trying to find a way to go on. I told the captain I would change names and details in the interests of people's privacy. He wanted to remain anonymous, and I said I'd do everything I could to achieve that. But I also said I wanted to share the essence of what I'd learned.

"I want people to know about these guys," I told him.

"Yeah," he said. "So do I."

I went home and started to write. I would start my days at the office, go home and, with my husband, feed our children and put them to bed, and then end up at the computer, writing into the small hours of the morning. I only wrote at night, liberated by the license of sleep deprivation. I have never written anything in such an uninterrupted fashion. No outline, few preconceptions, no notion of what would be the beginning, middle, or end. I just typed forward. I think it helped that I had no certainty it would ever be produced.

I am a compulsive note-taker at all times, and I had been one through the fall of 2001 as well. I had pages of legal pads filled with quotes, facts, and expressions that puzzled or pleased me, all in what I had come to think of as the metallic music of firehouse speech. Above all, I wanted to capture that voice, because I thought it was beautiful and because it expressed humor and compassion in such a natural and unexpected way. I tried to protect individuals from unwanted publicity by changing everything I could: names, places, physical characteristics. I fictionalized details in some places and created composite characters in others. But sometimes the material defeated my intentions.

When I came to write about the tool bench in the firehouse, nothing would do but to write about the tool bench. And so the tool bench remained.

I also thought about changing a reference to my own home state, Oklahoma. But I wanted to preserve the unspoken resonance of the Oklahoma City bombing, which had shaken us all so deeply and yet was now dwarfed by this even more catastrophic event.

A little over a week later, I e-mailed a draft of the play to Jim. I called him the next day, saying that I had to fly to Barcelona to give a lecture. I would welcome his comments so that I could work on a rewrite on the plane. "Take the weekend off," he said.

When I got back, Jim said he wanted to produce it. I was taken aback. I called the captain, who had not expected anything to be written so quickly. He came up to my apartment, and my husband and I read the play aloud to him. "Do it," he said. "It's what happened." He asked me to make two changes—nothing I would ever have expected, but points that were sensitive to firehouse culture. I made the changes instantly.

Jim had asked me if I had any problem with the idea of his wife, Sigourney Weaver, playing the role of the editor. Dream on, I thought. "No problem," I answered. In short order, I was told that she had contacted her friend Bill Murray about playing the fire captain. The four of us met in Jim and Sigourney's living room several times a week, with Bill and Sigourney reading over the piece, making minor adjustments, and letting it sink in. The three of them brought acute intelligence and an instant, fierce commitment to the project. I cannot remember any collaboration, at any point in my career, being as satisfying as this one. We sat in that light-flooded room over a dozen November mornings and I, as a first-time playwright, listened as they breathed life into the words of *The Guys*.

We all wanted the play to open soon. Jim decided to stage the piece as a workshop, with scripts on music stands, in a form that had been developed by A. R. Gurney in *Love Letters*. Jim is a brilliantly minimalist director, and settled on a production with few props, a set made up of little more than a pair of chairs and a table. The dominant colors were magenta and cobalt. The effect was of something glowing. I told friends not to expect any recent trends from the theater—no sex, no violence, no obscenity. The "special effects" consisted of turning the lights on and the captain putting on a hat.

Only days before *The Guys* was scheduled to open, I realized that we didn't have the rights to the music for the tango and there was no time to obtain them. A tune came into my head one day on the subway, no doubt the fruit of my affection for Argentina and the music of Carlos Gardel. I jotted it down in my notebook and invited my son's violin teacher, Nathan Lanier, to help with an arrangement. He brought some friends to the theater the next afternoon and they recorded it as a string trio. Somehow it was all in the spirit of the work.

The Guys premiered as a workshop production at the Flea Theater in New York with Sigourney Weaver and Bill Murray. It opened on Tuesday, December 4, 2001, twelve weeks to the day after the World Trade Center attack.

Contents

Director's Note

The Guys, by Anne Nelson, was commissioned by the Flea Theater in October 2001 in response to the events of September 11.

The Flea is a tiny theater located in TriBeCa, some blocks away from Ground Zero. The week before September 11, the Flea had five plays in repertory, two dance companies in residence, and a popular concert series. Then the entire neighborhood was closed and our activities ceased. When we were able to reopen, a month later, our attendance dropped by 90 percent. Not only did our neighborhood still reek of smoke and ash, but the community was traumatized. What was entertaining before that Tuesday now seemed irrelevant. Our little theater clearly was going to join the list of business casualties resulting from 9/11.

A member of our resident company suggested that we find or create a piece that would speak to what had happened to us. I have always felt that theater is an immediate art; but as I told this young native New Yorker, that is easier said than done. After all, this was a catastrophic event, with so many deaths, so much grief, so much uncertainty.

Shortly thereafter, though, I met Anne Nelson at a dinner for the Lawyers Committee for Human Rights. Nelson, who teaches at the Columbia Graduate School of Journalism, had never written a play, but she agreed to weave various experiences and ideas relating to the attack into a play that would address the theater's needs. *The Guys* was written in the midnight hours in a little more than a week.

In December 2001, *The Guys* opened with Sigourney Weaver and Bill Murray. We began our outreach to specific communities and gave free performances to firefighters and students. Six months later, *The Guys* continues to play to full houses. The list of prominent actors who've joined us includes Anthony LaPaglia, Susan Sarandon, Bill Irwin, Tim Robbins, Swoosie Kurtz, Amy Irving, and Tom Wopat. Like the character Joan, they've answered the play's call to use their "tools" to respond.

When the Flea found itself threatened, we rediscovered the theater's ability to respond in an immediate and direct fashion.

JIM SIMPSON
Artistic Director, the Flea Theater
May 2002

Author's Note

For readers outside New York City, it may be helpful to know that Mark Green was a Democratic candidate for mayor. He first ran in the primary on September 11. That had to be rescheduled, and there was a run-off before he was finally defeated in the November election by Republican Michael Bloomberg.

Rent stabilization is a regulation that affects some apartments in New York, especially for tenants who have occupied the same unit for many years. Stabilized rents are usually well below market rates.

PART I

Are You Okay?

Opening Monologue

(A tall woman, simply dressed in pants; she stands, spotlit, at center stage and addresses the audience directly)

JOAN   New York. My beautiful, gleaming, wounded city.

When I was a little girl in Oklahoma, I'd wait every week for *Newsweek* and *Life* magazine to plop into the mailbox. What were they doing this week in New York City? Going to plays written by Eur-o-pee-ans. Listening to jazz and string quartets. All those things you weren't supposed to do in Oklahoma. I thought you probably needed a passport to get into New York. I had this picture in my mind of people lined up at the bridge, paying a fee for admission.

I was right.

I hit New York when I was seventeen. I never really went back. Stone by stone, I built my life. A prewar apartment on the Upper West Side.

(Conspiratorially) Rent-stabilized.

Filled with music and books. A husband who liked opera more than football. Two charming children in a good private school. An interesting job.

Oh yes, my career. I started out, as a young woman, traveling to Latin America and writing about the dirty wars. I was a brave, foolish twenty-five-year-old girl—yes, girl, though I would have fought that word at the time. I saw bodies, talked to refugees, dodged bombs. The only time I was really afraid was on nights before I got on the plane to go back down. I'd cut my deal with God. If I got killed this time, someone would have to feed my cat.

That was before I had human dependents.

After a few years, I burned out. I settled down. I made my mother happy. And when I got my normal life, my apartment, my family, it was like a gift. Every time I took a hot shower I was grateful. Gradually, I stopped reporting. I found work as an editor. I became—theoretical.

(Beat)

"Where were you September eleventh?" Question of the year. I was at home, getting ready to go vote for Mark Green.

How many times did I vote for Mark Green? It was like Catholics and the weekly obligation.

The phone rings and it's my father in Oklahoma, "Is your TV on?" "No," I want to say. "Only people in Oklahoma have their TVs on at nine o'clock in the morning."

(Changes demeanor to talking-to-father mode)

"No," I say. "Why?" "A plane crashed into the World Trade Center. Musta been one of those little planes, pilot had a heart attack." "Dad," I said. "Maybe it's terrorism." He thought about it. "Why would someone do that?"

(Long beat)

So I turned on the television and joined the witnesses of the world. I called my husband, who works on Thirty-first Street. So he could tell his office mates and they could all go watch it out the window.

Note this—my dad calls from Oklahoma so I can call my husband so he can watch it out the window.

That moment marked the end of the Post-Modern Era.

So we all, in our assigned places, watch the second plane hit. We watch the towers go down.

And then, because I don't know what else to do, I go to the corner polling place and vote for Mark Green . . .

The week after the attack, I visit my sister in Park Slope. She lives in Park Slope because she's ten years younger than me. Over the ten years between us, the Upper West Side got priced out of the market.

I like Park Slope. It's more like my neighborhood used to be.

They just had another kid, three months old, and I needed to hold that baby. It was primal. That week you could have scored big in the rent-a-baby trade.

The phone rang; my sister answered. It was her friend the masseuse. Park Slope—you have friends who are masseuses. You meet them at the bookstore coffee shop during poetry readings.

This friend was giving emergency massages to rescue workers. Look, she said. I've been working on this guy. Bad shape. He's a fire captain, and he just lost most of his men. He's got to give the eulogies. The first one is on Thursday. He—can't write them. He needs a writer.

Well, I said. When was the last time I heard someone say they *needed* a writer? In fact, that was just when we were all discovering our "crisis of marginality."

Everyone wanted to help. But we couldn't. They didn't want amateurs wandering around the site. They didn't want our blood. Even surgeons felt useless. A friend of mine went to volunteer. Plumbers and carpenters first, they said. Intellectuals to the back of the line.

The firefighter needs a writer.

I called him. He lived down the block. Come now, I said. I have a few hours. My sister took the baby out for the day.

I knew exactly what to expect. Fire captain. Big guy. Works out.

(A knock. Lights come up to reveal a modest living room. There are two chairs with side tables that hold a coffee pot, half full, and two cups. It is early afternoon. Over the course of the play, the lights gradually dim toward evening)

(JOAN walks stage right to meet NICK. He is in his late forties, no taller than JOAN. He is informally dressed. He

holds a folder of files in his hand. He looks around him uncertainly, with an apologetic, disoriented expression, then offers his hand. They shake)

NICK   Joan?

JOAN   Hi.

NICK   Hi.

JOAN   I . . . I'm really sorry about . . . what happened.

NICK   *(Unfocused gaze)* Oh. Yeah. *(Comes back into focus and looks at her anxiously)* Look, I feel really bad about this. It's a beautiful afternoon. It's the weekend. You should be with your kids. You don't need to be doing this.

JOAN   My kids have play dates. I'm useless. It's fine. Hey, do you want some coffee?

NICK   Yeah, sure, if you've got some going.

JOAN   *(She gets up)* Milk? Sugar?

NICK   Just black.

(She goes to the kitchen and brings back two mugs, handing him one. They sit down, and he puts the files down on the table. They look down at their cups in silence)

NICK   See, I just don't know what to do. These guys . . . the call came, and they went off, and . . . they haven't found them yet but . . . some of the families, they want to have the service now so they can try to move on . . . I got to get up and talk in church . . . I been sitting down in front of a piece of paper all day, and I haven't been able to write one sentence. Not a thing—I keep going into a clutch. *(He looks at her helplessly)* I mean, I'm no writer under normal circumstances. But now . . . What can I tell the families? What am I going to say?

JOAN Hey, it's okay. Maybe I can help. I . . . I've never written a eulogy before, but I've written some speeches. It's okay. Now, how many did you say there were?

NICK *(He sighs)* Eight.

JOAN Eight.

NICK Eight men. I lost eight men.

JOAN So . . . eight eulogies. *(She stares at the paper in front of her)* Well, we'll just take it a step at a time, do what we can. You say that one of the services is next week?

NICK Yeah, Thursday.

JOAN So we'll do that one first.

NICK You see, the department has almost 350 men unaccounted for. It's been twelve days, but they haven't found any bodies. Some of the families, they're still waiting, they say they're going to find them alive in some air pocket or something. But the other families, they say no, they're gone. They want to go ahead and have the service. But they don't have bodies.

JOAN *(Slowly, taking it in)* Right.

NICK Some of the families are putting a picture up where the coffin is supposed to go. And we'll just do the eulogies up there with the photograph.

JOAN Uh-huh.

NICK . . . but the thing is, we're talking about 350 men—you got to understand, over a bad year we might lose maybe . . . six. This was in one day. One hour.

(Pause)

So. That means 350 services. But if they keep digging and find some bodies, the families might want funerals to bury them, and if every guy had a service *and* a funeral, that would be 700 . . . We'll be doin' this for a year. *(Thinks for a moment)* I hope they don't all want funerals too. *(She shakes her head, absorbing the thought)*

(They sit silently)

JOAN So which services are scheduled so far?

NICK *(Pause while he tries to think)* I've got the list here. *(He opens the file and looks through several papers)* Bill Dougherty, he's first. That's Thursday. Then Jimmy Hughes. He's the next week. After that there's Patrick O'Neill. That's a real hard one. My best friend. What a fine man. His wife wants to do his on his birthday. And the next day is Barney Keppel. Barney. Everybody loved Barney. The guys are going to take that one hard.

JOAN   *(She writes the names on a list and looks at it)* So that makes four we need to do today. Well, we'll just try it a step at a time. Thursday?

NICK   Thursday. Yeah. Bill Dougherty.

JOAN   *(She sits with pen poised over notepad)* Catholic service?

(NICK nods mutely)

JOAN   Did you talk to the priest? Do you know how long the eulogy's supposed to be?

NICK   Oh, not too long. Four minutes, five max. No, not even that long. There'll be other people talking too. But the families want me to say something. I'm the captain. What can I say to them? How can I explain it?

JOAN   Hey, it's okay . . . *(Softly)* I mean . . .

(She reaches a hand toward his shoulder, but awkwardly withdraws it; he doesn't see. She fetches a box of paper

tissues, puts them unobtrusively on the table, and sits down. He takes one and grips it tightly in his hand)

JOAN Human beings have been giving eulogies for thousands of years. You're doing this for the families. You'll comfort them. It's for them. It won't be about what happened that day. We'll talk about who they were, make it about them. That's what you can give the families.

NICK I keep hearing all these speeches from the politicians on TV. The pictures in the papers. Hero this, hero that. I don't even recognize them.

JOAN So that's why it's good *you're* doing this. You can give their families and friends something they can recognize. You can do that. So, hey, tell me about Bill.

NICK *(He takes a deep breath)* Bill. Yeah, Bill. Well, see, that's the problem. There's just not much to say. This hero stuff, like they were some guys in a movie. But Bill—he wasn't like that. He was just an ordinary guy. A schmo. If Bill walked into a room, nobody would even notice. *(Looks up to her helplessly)* You can't say that in a eulogy.

JOAN Hey, it's okay. Don't worry. We'll do this. I mean, people who are ordinary . . . in a . . . an extraordinary situation—that's what this is about. Now back up a little bit. Tell me about him. What did he look like? When you think of him, what comes to your mind?

NICK   Look like? He looked like—a plumber. Not a big guy. Reddish hair. Mid-forties. But he was the senior man. All the junior men relied on him. They had their eyes on him to know what to do. "My men," he called them.

JOAN   When you close your eyes, where do you see him? What's he doing?

NICK   *(Thinks)* In the kitchen.

JOAN   The kitchen?

NICK   The guys spend a lot of time in the kitchen between runs. There's a lot of downtime. Bill's there saying, "I'm looking out for my men . . . my men need this . . ." Yeah, Bill spent a lot of time talking in the kitchen. He was real good with the younger guys. He was always taking them and pointing things out to them.

JOAN   *(Writing it down, encouragingly)* Uh-huh . . . yeah?

NICK   See, someone like Bill—he's real senior; he's been there sixteen years. There's always new guys comin' through, and sometimes they can be a pain in the ass for the older guys. They're a little nervous, and they don't know where things are. A guy like Bill could have blown them off, but he was always lookin' out for them. Here's the gear, here's the tools, here's how you handle it, no, not like that, like this . . .

JOAN   *(Writing)* Was he a family man? Religious?

NICK   Oh, Bill was quiet. Never talked about himself. Half the company didn't even know he was married. I know he went to mass, but he never made a show of it. But he was proud of being Irish. You know, I think that's why he was a fireman—it's thick in the Irish blood.

(Pause)

He loved New York, all its nooks and crannies. You know, these guys see the city from the outside and the inside, underground and in all the hidden places. Bill wanted to know the history of everything. I remember him telling me, "Nick, just got this great book— *A Walking Tour of Flatbush Avenue.*"

JOAN   Flatbush Avenue!

NICK   You want to have a guy like that around, especially downtown, with all these crazy streets. Nowadays, you get a computerized map when you get a call. But somebody can still call in and give you bad directions, or a building name with no address, or no entrance on that side of the street . . .

JOAN   I never thought of that.

NICK   On that day . . . I still don't know what happened. I can't find anyone who saw the company.
They got off the apparatus and the officer told the
driver, "We're going to Tower One." They're running
down West Street in full gear about the time the second plane hit. And maybe they peeled off and went to
Tower Two. But we don't know where to look for
them. *(Stops, choked)*

JOAN   *(After a moment)* What else did Bill love? Any
sports? Music? You said he hung out in the kitchen—
did he like to cook?

NICK   Oh, Bill wasn't exactly a cook. The guys take
turns making meals for everybody. Sometimes it's
okay, but it can get pretty bad. I call their cooking
"valiant attempts and dismal failures."

JOAN   *(She smiles)* Yeah?

NICK   Every guy has his specialty, and they usually
cook it every time it's their turn. We're talking under-
cooked chicken and *nasty* Rice-A-Roni. Bill would sit
there and try it, and come up with some real zingers.

JOAN   So he was more of a critic.

NICK   Yeah, yeah!—he was the firehouse food critic.
And he could zap 'em but good. But not mean. He
was never mean.

JOAN   Okay, okay . . . Yeah, this is good. This works.
'Cause you know, Nick, you want to give people

someone they recognize. Not just a plaster saint. This is good. Wait a minute. *(She writes, crosses out, draws some arrows on the page)*

NICK   *(Watching her)* I'm really sorry. I'm not giving you anything to work with here. I shouldn't be doing this to you.

JOAN   *(Still focused on the paper, shaking her head)* No, no, just wait. *(She tears off a sheet, copies from one sheet to another, then quickly numbers paragraphs)* Here. *(She hands two pages to NICK)* Try this. Start here, and it jumps to there. And . . . if you could read it out loud so I can hear it?

NICK   *(Reads slowly)* "I'm Nick Flanagan, captain of Ladder Company 60. I've worked with Bill Dougherty for a long time. I want to give my condolences to all of Bill's family here with us today."

(Nods) Okay.

(He resumes reading) "We've been hearing a lot about heroes, and Bill was one of them. He gave his life for others, and that is a noble thing. But Bill was a quiet hero. Never one to show off, never blustered. He was a firefighter for sixteen years, and he was a good one. He had the most important quality for a firefighter. He was absolutely dependable." *(He looks up and smiles at her)* Yeah. That's right. Dependable.

(He continues reading) "Over time, we realized how important he was for the newer guys at the firehouse. Sometimes it can be hard for the experienced men to show the young ones the drills year after year. But Bill was always looking out for the new guys, showing them the ropes. And he did it in that quiet way of his, never made them feel small. 'My men,' he called them. 'My men.' " *(Looks at her)* Yeah. You got it. You got it. That's him.

JOAN   They're your words. I just put them in order.

NICK   No. You got the craft. You know how to put it.

(He reads on) "He was like an older brother to them, looking out for them. They appreciated it, and I appreciated it. You got to have guys like Bill to build a strong team. They may not say much, but they hold things together.

"If Bill hadn't been a fireman, he could have been a food critic. Bill used to spend a lot of time in the kitchen, talking to the guys and evaluating the cuisine. When Bill tried out a questionable dish, he could come up with some real zingers. The restaurants of New York are lucky he went into another line of work."

Yeah. The guys'll like that. *(Nods. Looks from one page to the next, finds his place)* "What did Bill love?

He loved his family, and he loved this city. On September eleventh, he was the senior man. The younger men could look to someone who was steady and professional, to show the way. We know that Bill and the other firefighters of New York saved thousands of lives that day. That means that there are thousands of people and their family members who are able to go on because of them. We can only thank them and ask for God's kindest blessing on those they have left behind." *(He absorbs it)*

JOAN *(She pauses and looks at him anxiously)* So it works?

NICK You got it. I can do this. I'll have this in front of me when I get up there, something to give them.

*(*JOAN *takes a breath, closes her eyes, and slumps back into her chair)*

NICK You okay?

*(*JOAN *stands up)*

Monologue II

JOAN *(Addressing the audience)* "Are you okay?" That was what we all kept asking each other the rest of

September. What was the answer? The pebble's dropped in the water. The point of entry is you, yourself. Were you present at ground zero and wounded, suffocated, or covered in white ash? No? I guess you're okay.

The first ring around the pebble: "Is your family okay?" Did you lose someone in the towers or on the planes?

The next ripple—friends. "Are your people okay?"

Next ripple: If someone died in the tower that you had dinner with once and thought was a really nice person, are you okay?

Next: If you look at a flyer of a missing person in the subway and you start to lose it, are you okay?

(Pause)

If all the flyers are gone one day. They're—gone. Are you okay?

Is anyone okay?

That first week I bought a coffee at Starbucks on the way to work, and the guy at the counter handed me my cup and said, "Here's your change. God bless

America." And I took a breath, and said, "Are your people okay?" And he said, "Only two missing." Only two. And I said . . . *(In strained voice)* "I hope you can find comfort."

Only people from Oklahoma talk to servers in coffee shops. But at least there you can say, "God bless." Here, you don't know if they have a God, or if you have a God—or if *anyone* has a God, it's the same God. That wants the same things . . .

We all travel in our track: neighborhood, job, friends. Parents of your children's friends. No matter how big a city gets, the only way to live in it is to live in your village. You get to a certain age, the next person you meet has a logical connection to the ones that came before. Friend of a friend.

Nick and I weren't supposed to meet. You couldn't create another sequence for his life that leads to me. Or for my life that leads to him. After September eleventh, all over the city, people were jumping tracks.

PART II

Pain Has Its Price

(NICK and JOAN are back in their places)

NICK Jimmy. What can I say about Jimmy? He was the new guy. Still on probation. I hardly knew the guy. I never even got to meet his family. His girlfriend came down to the firehouse last week. Nice girl. Said he was a bicycle racer. The bike club out in Flushing had a memorial for him, put flowers on the handlebars and everything. *(He stops short)* But that's all I know about him.

JOAN How long was he there?

NICK Oh, he was only with the ladder company for a couple of weeks. He had been with the engine company for seven weeks before that. That's what they do with the probies—seven weeks engine, seven weeks ladder. But when they flip 'em to ladder, they come into my office the first day, we shake hands, and then we might not see each other that much for a while.

JOAN Ladder?

NICK The ladder company. See, there are two companies side by side. The mission of the engine is to put water on the fire. They got the hoses, they work like a team to get it where it has to go. Ladder—we do ventilation, entry, and search.

JOAN *(Feeling a little slow)* So your engine has the ladder thing.

NICK No, no. You call the engine an engine and the ladder a truck. Oh yeah, the big ladder, sure. But a lot of other things too. All kinds of ladders. Suitcase ladder—beautiful, folds up so you can carry it like a suitcase. Axes. Electronic sensors. We got the forcible-entry team that breaks down the doors so the guys with the hoses can get in. Engine and truck, we work out of the same firehouse, and sometimes we hang out together, but we don't know all each others' guys the same way.

JOAN I see. So Jimmy just got there. What was it like for him?

NICK *(Struggling)* He had to learn fast. He was willing to learn—it was always, "Show me more, show me more." I think he had a lot of friends that were firemen.

JOAN How old was he?

NICK I got it here. *(He opens the file in front of him and leafs through a couple of pages, squinting)* I think ... let's see ... Yeah, he was ... uh, twenty-six.

JOAN   Oh. *(She writes slowly)* What kind of things did he like? What did he look like?

NICK   *(He turns the pages in the file slowly, in consternation)* I don't know, I just don't know. He wasn't there that long. And with everything that's happened . . . *(He looks at her desperately)* This is terrible. This is a terrible thing. But I have to tell you— right now, I can't even remember his face. *(He is anguished and ashamed)*

JOAN   Hey. Hey. We'll do this. We'll figure it out. *(She studies her notes)* Now, you say they come into your office on the first day.

NICK   Yeah, they all do. They come in, and I shake their hand, and I say, "Welcome to the company. This is the best job in the world." *(He stops)* Two weeks before this happened, I shook his hand. But I didn't tell him he'd be dead.

JOAN   *(Gently)* You didn't know. *(He's still silent)* So how was he doing at the job?

NICK   I'm not real sure. He was still learning.

JOAN   I mean, if he was screwing up, you would have heard about it, right?

NICK   Oh yeah. I always hear about it if they screw up. *(Pause while he thinks)* I didn't hear anything like that.

JOAN   *(Writing)* So he wasn't screwing up. So he was

doing fine. And he went through probation, and every guy goes through probation, so we can put that in, too, right?

NICK   *(Tentatively)* Yeah . . .

JOAN   So how does it work?

NICK   Well, first they got to take the test. And then there's this brutalizing physical. And paperwork, lots of paperwork. Piles of paperwork. And then they go home and wait. Long, long wait. They think it'll never end. Most of the guys get rejected. But if you're lucky, you get the call. "This is Fireman So-and-so. Come on down. You're in."

JOAN   *(Writing and smiling)* Yeah. And then what?

NICK   And then you start. And you sit down, keep your eyes open, and shut up.

JOAN   Right. What are the senior guys like with the new ones?

NICK   Well, you know. They show 'em around. Some are more patient than others. They give 'em a little bit of a hard time. Not exactly hazing—it all goes with the territory. Jimmy was doing fine. He was a regular guy, low-key. Well liked. He came in same time with another probie. Hipólito Díaz. I love that name. You gotta love that name. Where do they get these names? Sounds like a ballpark. Put him in the outfield. *(He assumes a sports-announcer voice)*

"Now batting for Mariano Rivera, Hipólito Díaz."
(Pause) Hippo's missing too. He's missing with the
guys from the engine.

JOAN *(Long beat)* So they started in the summer, right?
Was it a long, hot summer? What was it like in the
firehouse in the weeks leading up to it?

NICK Oh, nothing special. Some little stuff. False
alarms, wastebasket fires. The guys were a little rest-
less. This was the day. They were chomping at the bit.
This was the day they were waiting for.

JOAN So Jimmy hadn't really been in many fires
before.

NICK No, no, this was it. September eleventh. *(He
shakes his head slightly in wonder. He is shocked at
the realization)* This was his first real fire.

*(*JOAN *stands up)*

Monologue III

JOAN *(Addressing the audience—angry)* Of course,
everyone has their own description. Myself, I favor
the idea that it's like a massive boot, stomping right
here. *(She thumps her outstretched hands across her
chest and diaphragm. Struggles to take a deep breath)*
Knocks the wind out. *Heartbreak* sounds too deli-
cate, too pretty for this sensation. It's a body blow.

And then you just can't breathe, not really. Not for a long time.

(She assumes a pedagogical voice) Brain Chemistry for Dummies: Lesson One: The science of pain.

(She's in a pseudo–medical authoritative demeanor. She picks up a book, opens it, and reads from it) "Cortisol is released in response to stress. Cortisol is sometimes called a 'stress hormone.' A variety of psychological stressors can cause cell death in the nerves affected by the cortisol system. . . ." *(She shakes her head)* Cell death. Don't like *that*.

"Trauma is translated into anatomical changes in the brain. . . . Stress can cause changes in the neural architecture—the hard wiring—of the brain. . . . Diminished blood flow to the brain causes comparable brain-cell death. And so does normal aging." *(She looks at the audience. Bitter) That* explains a lot.

Put simply: We've got nerve fibers running through our brains like lines strung across telephone poles. Our brain sends out chemical messages that leap from pole to pole. And when we experience devastation—trauma—toxins spill out and . . .

God, can you imagine what it looks like in there?

(She stops short. Then she resumes reading) "When monkeys are subjected to severe forms of stress, they show signs like passivity, cries of distress, and self-directed behaviors like huddling and rocking . . ." *(She absorbs it)* ". . . The animal model seems to say that pain has its price. The victim carries his scars."

(She closes the book. The lights come up on the stage, and she takes her place in the chair at the table, where NICK *is still sitting)*

JOAN   Here. Try this. *(She hands* NICK *her notebook)*

NICK   *(He traces the sentences with his finger, reading through the boilerplate passage sotto voce)* "I'm Nick Flanagan of Ladder Company 60 . . ." Yeah. "Honor the memory . . . condolences . . ." Okay, here.

(More formally) "Jimmy's job was to learn as much as possible, as fast as possible. We could tell he was going to be good. He was quiet, helpful, and hardworking. The guys liked him, and they're good judges of character." *(Pause)* Yeah, this is working.

(He resumes reading) "On that morning in September, Jimmy was going out on his first big fire. He was

serving with the cream of the crop, and he was holding his own. They were ready for this day. It was the work they had chosen, work that was about risking everything—risking your life—in order to save others. In our grief, let us remember that." *(He nods to himself)*

"When Jimmy first came to the firehouse, he came into my office and I shook his hand, telling him what I tell all the new men. 'This is the best job in the world.' Now I would say, 'This is the most important job in the world.' "

(He's shaken by this, and she's distressed. They sit quietly and motionlessly)

JOAN   I . . . I'm sorry. Maybe that last part's not right.

NICK   *(Staring into the middle distance)* "The best job in the world." Can I say that in front of his folks? *(He looks at her)* But it's true! I've been doing it for more than twenty years. I can't imagine doing anything else.

JOAN   I believe you.

NICK   These guys, you just wouldn't believe these guys.

JOAN   *(A long beat)* More coffee?

NICK   Why not.

JOAN   *(She takes his cup and refills it)* Here you go. It's a little cold.

NICK   You should try the coffee at the firehouse. It's really bad.

JOAN   Oh, I drink a lot of bad coffee.

NICK   No, I mean really bad. *(He grins)* Disgusting.

JOAN   *(Smiling)* I usually don't drink it this late in the day anyway.

NICK   *(He's suddenly anxious, looks around)* It is getting late. Hey, I should be getting outa here. It's your weekend. You got plenty of other things you need to do.

JOAN   Nick, when we were talking on the phone, I thought about what I was going to do this afternoon. Nothing more important than this. But next week, once I'm in the office, with the kids and everything— then it might be hard to get back. Let's see what we can do today.

NICK   Patrick. We got to do Patrick. The thing is, I think I'm—what do they call it—denial, in denial about Patrick. I swear, I'm sitting in the office and the door opens and I think he's gonna walk in.

JOAN   *(She looks down at her notes)* Patrick O'Neill.

NICK   Oh, Patrick. This man had a full, full life. This man always had something going on. His work, his family, his church. I say to him one time, "What are you doin' this weekend?" And he says, "Going to the church picnic." I didn't know they still *had* church picnics!

JOAN Kids?

NICK Four. Christie, she just got married. I think she's twenty-five. The twins, they're fourteen. And Theresa's ten. Wife Mary Rose. He's got a birthday coming up, he's gonna be forty-seven next month.

JOAN How long was he with the company?

NICK Patrick came into the company as a brand-new lieutenant four years ago. I got to see this man grow. When you're new you're shaky about everything, but over time I saw him grow. He had conviction—that was the thing about Patrick. He knew this was the job for him. He was sure he could do it. That's what makes a leader. The troops eat it up.

JOAN So the men looked up to him.

NICK Oh yeah. So they wanted to follow. That's the difference between being a boss and a leader. Patrick was six weeks away from taking his captain's test. No doubt about it, he had it.

JOAN Are the men ever—afraid?

NICK Afraid. People are afraid, but they never admit it.

JOAN You can't admit it. Everything would fall apart. You can't afford that.

NICK   They need someone to follow. Good decisions. Calm under fire. I don't like the cowboy hotshot type, never did. Pat wasn't like that. When I think of him, I think of when I was in the army infantry. They had this motto: "Follow me." That's what he was like. Confident. "Follow me." And they did. *(He pauses briefly)* That morning, too.

JOAN   What picture do you have of him? When you think about him, what do you see him doing?

NICK   Oh, I see him walking. With these giant strides— you're not gonna stop *this* train. He could cover a room in two steps. Yeah, I see him leading five guys up to a building, sizing it up—first thing he does when he gets to a fire, walk around, size it up. And these five guys behind him, running to keep up. And all the time they're listening to him, thinking, What does he want? How do we do this job right?

JOAN   How does he motivate them? Criticism or praise?

NICK   Oh, there's lots of praise, back in the kitchen. But he kept an eye on them too, especially the new guys, the probies. "This one's good," he'd say if he liked him. But don't try to pull anything over on him. If you got a square-rooter, Pat picked up on that right away. He knew.

JOAN   A square-rooter?

NICK   That's what we call them—a guy that's just out for himself. You know, an operator.

JOAN   So Patrick was a real straight arrow.

NICK   Oh yeah. "Work, church, and home." That was the motto. He was a real role model for the men. Last year, when Barney Keppel had his little brush with the law, Patrick helped him out. Barney goes to him and says, "Okay, Lieutenant, from now on, I'm a new man. Work, church, and home. Just like you."

JOAN   He must have liked that.

NICK   Oh yeah. He didn't believe it—not for a minute. Barney was "work, church, and home"—at least until Friday. Maybe Thursday. But that was okay. Barney didn't mean any harm; he just got into scrapes. Him and Dave. Barney and Dave.

JOAN   So Patrick talked a lot about his kids?

NICK   Oh yeah. It was always "I got Frankie's soccer practice this weekend, gonna meet Christie's in-laws on Sunday, tonight we're going to Theresa's recital." This man had a full life. One day he says, "I made Waldorf salad for the church picnic. You gotta try it sometime." He goes to the church picnic. I tell you, I didn't know they *had* church picnics anymore. *(He shakes his head in wonder)*

JOAN   Well, I can't say that I've been to any lately.

NICK   *(Mournfully)* Nobody's having any fun anymore.

JOAN   We're all walking under this cloud.

(There's a silence. Then she brightens)

But there was something last night. A tango wedding party. No, really, I went to a tango wedding party. Only in New York. He's Japanese, she's a blonde from California, and they met at their tango club in Central Park.

The party was in this restaurant down on Thirty-eighth Street. The whole place was done up all white and silver, with candlelight. They had a little tango trio—real Argentines. And they played, and after the dinner people danced—ten couples, the bride and groom. They were really good!

NICK   Tango. That's a difficult dance.

JOAN   And the women were all dressed up, with their hair up, wearing little high-heeled shoes with pointy toes. You don't see that anymore. When they got going on the dance floor, their feet just flashed. It was so beautiful. It was like a dream intermission in the middle of—all this.

And there was drama, too. On the eleventh, the groom was flying in from the West Coast, and the bride was working downtown. And there were hours and hours when each one thought the other one was dead. But they weren't. So they had this incredible evening. It was beautiful. They were beautiful. They made us all beautiful. For a few hours.

NICK I dance, you know. That's my big thing.

JOAN You dance? Really?

NICK Yeah. I've been taking lessons for years. I don't do the competitions. I just like learning new stuff and perfecting my steps. And the people—the people are great.

JOAN What kind of dancing?

NICK Lots of kinds. Swing, ballroom. Tango is the top dance—that's really at the top. Very difficult dance. You can study tango for a long time. You like to dance?

JOAN Oh, I like to. But my husband doesn't, so I don't get the chance. But watching them made me want to. Their teachers were there—I never saw dancing like that before.

NICK Usually you don't get to dance with your teacher socially. But once we were at this party and my teacher said, "Yeah, c'mon, let's do it." What an experience. You looked at her, and it was all there— the frame. She was perfect—you can't make a mistake when you're dancing with perfection.

JOAN The frame?

NICK   The frame. *(He demonstrates)* It's the invisible box you're standing in, and how you hold yourself inside it.

JOAN   *(Uncomprehendingly)* Oh.

NICK   Like, if you push your partner's hand—here, give me your hand— *(She remains seated. He takes her right hand with his left, in ballroom posture)* If you push your partner's hand . . . *(He pushes her hand, palm to palm, and it gives way easily)* . . . and it's like cooked spaghetti, that's no good. Here, put up your hand again. *(She does, and he takes it. This time it's firm but pliant)* You gotta have some resistance. You got to feel the whole body move in the same direction. Cha, like this. *(Now when he pushes, her torso turns a bit to the side)* Otherwise it's no good. *(They drop hands, smiling self-consciously)*

JOAN   Yeah, I see.

NICK   And if you're lucky, it all comes together. When people move in synch. Sometimes it's real hard for these modern women, you know. They're professionals, they're educated, they're used to being in charge. But when you're dancing, you got to be able to follow. You've got to be able to feel the lead.

JOAN   You've got to let go.

NICK   Yeah. It's not so hard. You just follow. Here, like this.

(He gently takes her hand. The lights slowly dim, except for a spot on them. Soft music rises—a few strings playing "Hiro's Tango")

NICK   You know, there are only eight steps to the basic tango. Just lean into me, feel where I'm going. Yeah—step step cross step, step step step foot up. There you go, you're getting it.

(They go through the steps several times. They do not hold each other close. Their posture is slightly formal but friendly. At first he is encouraging and she is tentative and awkward in the steps.)

NICK   Don't look down.

(After a few tries, it becomes smoother, more fluid—but never melodramatic. The dance becomes more confident. Their movements synchronize. Then the music begins to fade. NICK retreats into the darkness to his chair. JOAN turns to the audience, still in the light)

Monologue IV

JOAN   *(Addressing the audience quietly)* Of course, that never happened. We didn't dance. He just gave my hand that little push, like the demonstration of a cantilever. It was all—proper. We never even got up from our chairs. But after that touch—whenever I watched him after that, I noticed how light he was on his feet. I could imagine him moving quickly and usefully across a landscape of flame and broken glass. I could see him at a dance class, swinging his partner, smiling as their steps snapped, synchronized, into place. I could see Jimmy Hughes, cresting a hill on his bike. And Patrick O'Neill with his kids and his salad at the picnic. It made me wonder what I used to *see* every time I walked past a firehouse. I never thought about a kitchen back there.

I knew then that every time I saw a person on the street, I saw only his public shadow. The rest, the important part, lies in layer after layer beyond our view.

We have no idea what wonders lie hidden in the people around us.

(JOAN *sits down in the dark, and the stage lights come up on the two of them*)

JOAN   Nick, where were you that morning?

NICK   At home. In Brooklyn. When it happened, I went outside to the street. I could see the towers on fire.

JOAN   You were off duty?

NICK   I wasn't due in until 6 P.M. that night. We work shifts. Patrick was on that morning.

JOAN   *(She's not writing. She's looking at him intently)*
You went to the firehouse?

NICK   *(Shaking his head slightly)* I made an entry in the
log at 10:15. I got there twenty minutes after the second tower went down . . .

(Long pause)

The engine and truck left at 8:52. We've got a video
camera at the door with a time clock. You see them
go out. We lost fourteen—eight from 60 Truck, six
from the engine. Two survived. Both drivers. One
driving the engine, one driving the truck. The last
thing Pat said was, "We're going into Tower One."

You see, there was a really stupid thing. You know
those big orange plastic cones they use for traffic?
Well, the ladder truck ran into one on the way, and it
got wedged under the fender. You can't go anywhere
till you get the cone out. Steve, the driver, he's out
there wrestling and cursing that cone, and it just
wouldn't come out. So Pat says, "Come on guys,
we'll go on, it's just a couple of blocks, and Steve can
meet us down there. We're going to Tower One."

Steve finally gets the cone out, and heads down. He
makes it to the lobby of Tower One, and he's trying
to find out where the company is. And then he's

blown out the lobby of Tower One by the collapse of Tower Two. He's blown clear out of that lobby. Hitting that stupid cone saved his life.

(They sit silently)

JOAN An orange plastic traffic cone.

NICK They still haven't found the guys. I don't know where they are. Maybe after the second plane hit Tower Two, they went there. I just have no idea. I keep trying to figure it out.

JOAN We can't figure any of this out. It's too big for us. People used to have religion. Something terrible would happen and they'd say, "Oh, it was God's will." But we don't . . . buy that now. God's will? This wasn't God's will. There's no reason. No explanation.

NICK Yeah. No reason. I say to Pat the night before, "You want to work first shift or second shift?" We do this all the time—trade off. And always before he has a reason. I'll take today, you take tomorrow. I'll take tomorrow, you take today. He'd say, "I got my daughter's soccer practice, I got this, I got that," there was always a reason. But that day, he just said, "Oh, I'll take Tuesday morning." This time he didn't give a reason. There's no reason. I'm alive and he's dead and I don't even know why. I lie awake nights thinking, What was the reason?

JOAN   No reason. *(She takes a drink of cold, bitter coffee, makes a face. Then she looks at her notes)* Nick, this guy sounds too perfect. I mean, he must have had some flaw. C'mon.

NICK   Flaw. *(He thinks hard)* Well, I guess he was a perfectionist.

JOAN   Okay.

NICK   *(He smiles)* It used to drive him nuts if something wasn't working right, if something was messy. If he saw the probies loafing around the firehouse: "Do something useful. Sweep or something!" Or if they were sitting in the kitchen. He'd say, "Don't just sit there. Read something!" That was Patrick.

JOAN   *(She smiles as she writes)* Yeah, okay. Is that a flaw . . . But at least it's human. We got to make him human.

NICK   *(Wistful)* I tell you, every day at the firehouse, I still think he's going to walk in that door.

JOAN   *(She reviews the page)* Tell me what you think of this. *(She stands up, holds the page before her, and reads aloud)* "I want to offer my condolences to his family, who are here with us today. It is impossible to think of Patrick without thinking of you. Even when he was working all-out, Patrick always had his family in mind." *(To NICK)* That's the sense I have of him.

NICK *(He nods with an expression of satisfaction)* Yeah, that's good.

JOAN "Patrick was a fine father. It was a quality he brought to the firehouse. He had that calm presence you look for in a leader. 'Follow me,' he'd say, and they would. The men looked up to him—for the way he did his job, but also for the way he lived his life. 'Work, church, and home' was his motto."

NICK *(He corrects her)* Well, that's what *Barney* always said was Patrick's motto. I don't know if that's what *Patrick* said was his motto. *(Thinks)* But no, no, leave it in, it sounds good.

JOAN "Patrick O'Neill was a big man. He covered the ground in long, sure strides. When he went out to a fire, he led the way. The other guys had to walk double-time just to keep up."

NICK That's right. I was one of them.

JOAN *(She looks at him inquiringly)* We could put that in.

(Pause) "He took special pride in the new guys, the probies. He expected the same sense of purpose in them that he had himself. If one of them was taking it easy around the firehouse and Patrick walked in, he'd need to find an emergency broom."

NICK That's good. "An emergency broom."

JOAN   *(She starts to read more haltingly, starts to have trouble)* "On September eleventh, Patrick was six weeks away from taking his captain's test, and there's no doubt about it. He would have aced it. When I think of Patrick, I think of the infantry motto 'Follow me.' I'm sure that's what Patrick said that morning when he got the alarm—'Follow me'—with his long stride that gave so much confidence and purpose to his men that day.

"And I don't care whether Patrick ever took that captain's test. In my book, he earned it. And captain's the least of it. Patrick O'Neill was many things to many people. Leader, friend, brother . . . husband, father . . . And none of us here will ever forget him."

(As she finishes, her voice starts to quaver. Her face is distorted. Perhaps she is in tears. NICK *is still listening, looking into an abstract distance. He turns to look at her after she finishes)*

NICK   That's . . . hey, what's . . . ? *(He stands up and makes a motion to comfort her but is uncertain what he should do. He regards her, awkward and distressed)* Aw, look what I've done. I've dragged you into this. I shouldn't a done that. I come along and unload all this stuff on you, and now you're wrecked too. I had no right to do that.

JOAN   No, you don't understand.

NICK   You're hurting. This hurts you.

JOAN   This is nothing, less than nothing, compared to what's happened to you.

NICK   That doesn't mean you should suffer.

JOAN   Can you use this? *(She holds up the paper)*

NICK   Yes. Yes! Now I'll have something to say when I get up there. And the words. They're the right words. But that doesn't mean I should drag you into this. You were outside of it, and I dragged you in.

JOAN   Was I outside of it? I don't want to be—not so far. This is my city, too. I can't just watch it on TV. I want to do something. But this is all I know how to do. Words. I can't think of anything else.

NICK   *(Wonderingly)* That's okay. They're your tools.

Monologue V

(The lights dim to a spotlight and JOAN *addresses the audience)*

JOAN   People need to tell their stories.

I know you absorb some toxins listening to the pain. It's like the print of a hand in raw clay. Even the people who tell the stories know this.

In Chile, some people who were tortured couldn't tell their families what happened. It caused the listeners too much pain. The people didn't want to hurt anyone with their stories—but they needed to tell them. So some shrinks gave them tape recorders and had them tell their stories to the machine. It helped.

You know, when it first happened, I'd wake up every day cleansed—of the memory. There would be these fresh moments after sleep. Then I'd remember. And another thought would resist: No; that's absurd. But the first thought would win. Yes, it happened, and now I have to go through another day living that reality.

I thought, It would be good to get away. So when they asked me to come to Argentina, I said yes. I was meeting with some Argentine writers. They told me what it all meant. "The United States is living under total military censorship," they said.

What?

"The military won't let the newspapers publish pictures of the bodies."

Wait, wait, I said. The newspapers—they're still trying to figure out what happened. What happens next. Pictures of the bodies? There aren't any bodies. Do you want pictures of pieces of bodies? Censorship—that's when information is blocked. They're not blocking that information. We know they're dead. People don't need pictures. People don't *need* pictures.

There was one woman in Argentina—her son was one of the disappeared there. She told the newspapers there that when the planes hit the towers she felt . . . glad. We all know who was in those towers, she said. American imperialists . . . had it coming. *(She shakes her head despairingly)* I wanted to tell her. *(Beat)* They were civilians. They were massacred. And if there's one thing we've salvaged from the bloody twentieth century, it's the idea of human rights. For everyone. Even Americans. *(Bitterly resolute)* Now, it may sound strange to talk about Americans as victims of a human-rights abuse. But. Strange. Things. Happen.

I couldn't wait to get back to New York. Where everyone understood. But I kept thinking about it. I realized that everything the Argentines were saying was about their own war twenty years ago. They thought it was about them. Everybody, all over the world, was talking about it. Writing about it. And they all—they all—thought it was about them! But it's not. It's about us!

Isn't it?

PART III

The Deal

(The light comes up on NICK *at the table.* JOAN *returns to her seat. The light in the room is dimmer)*

NICK   *(Glances toward the window)* It's getting dark.

JOAN   Yeah. *(She gets up and turns on a lamp)* We're rounding the bend.

NICK   You're tired. You're fried. I can tell by looking at you. Let's stop.

JOAN   *(Wearily)* One more. Didn't you say there's one more service scheduled?

NICK   Barney. Barney and Dave, my two wild men. But they haven't scheduled Dave.

JOAN   Okay, Barney. Tell me about Barney.

NICK   Oh, Barney. Everybody loves Barney. He and Dave were always getting into trouble.

JOAN   *(She writes. She's worn down)* Yeah?

NICK   See, these two guys had—*es*-ca-pades. Always together. *(Pause)* You know, Barney wasn't even supposed to work that morning—he just came down to the station to meet Dave. *(He grows expansive)* Dave. You wouldn't want to live next door to Dave, oh no. He had this house on Long Island. Yard full of old cars. He loved to mess around with wrecks. More wrecked, the better. So one day Dave hears about a '69 Thunderbird convertible in Wyoming. "I'm gonna go buy it," he tells us, and off he goes with Barney. These guys go driving their beat-up old T-bird cross country. They're supposed to be back at work, and we keep getting these calls—from South Dakota. Places like that. "Don' worry, Cap, we're coming, we're on our way." And afterwards they tell us the story. One of those firehouse tales in the kitchen, gets riper every time you hear it.

JOAN   So they fixed it up?

NICK   Oh yeah. Barney was a metalworker. He could do anything with metal. And a big sense of humor. He had this banter that kept you rolling. His jokes were pretty bad. And he would tell the same tired old one-liner over and over again. But somehow he always had everyone in stitches. Maybe it was the way he laughed at them himself. *(Shakes his head)* This was a guy that you loved.

JOAN   Popular.

NICK   Well—yes and no. You gotta understand, this was a guy in his mid-thirties. He still lived at home with his parents. An older couple. German. They never called him Barney. "Bernhardt," it was. *(He tries for a German accent)* His mom always said

"Bernhardt." Very orderly, very precise. Barney was like that. He had his own private workshop at the firehouse, did all the firehouse welding. He had all these tools. He collected old tools, machines from the twenties and thirties. He'd bring them in, nobody knows from where, nobody knew what they were for. Big things—drill presses, all kind of blades and stuff on them. Barney would take that old machinery, take it apart, clean it, and make it like new—and we still didn't know what it was for!

JOAN   My dad's like that.

NICK   Yeah? And, you know, up above the bench, where he hung his wrenches. Every tool had a spot on the wall with a . . . a . . . silhouette of the tool. It's that German precision. How did he get along with *Dave*? Dave's yard was a mess. Dave moves in next door, the property value goes down. That's what we always used to say.

JOAN   What did Barney look like?

NICK   Oh, you know, tall guy. Light hair. Kinda beefy. Not exactly handsome. He and Dave would go out drinking, try to meet some nice women, but Barney never had very good luck. Barney would say, if he could only meet a woman welder. That was the girl of his dreams. Whenever Barney met a new woman, the guys would say, "Yeah. But, Barney, can she weld?"

(A pause) Flashdance. That was his ideal woman.

JOAN   Was he a good fireman?

NICK   As a fireman? I thought he was real good. He was a man who worked with his hands, respected his tools. Asked questions. He knew what was going on . . . analytical. He was interested in everything. He took his talent and used it for the company.

JOAN   *(She writes with a little more energy)* Can you give me an example?

NICK   Let me think. Okay, we have this giant generator—power source. Took two guys to move it. Hurst Tool. You use it for traffic accidents.

JOAN   *(Taken aback)* Hearse tool? For hearses?

NICK   Hurst: *h-u-r-s-t*. Sometimes they call it "Jaws of Life," but it's a Hurst Tool. It's got these big jaws for cutting through metal, but it needs a lot of power. Generator weighs a ton, really hard to move around. So Barney takes his tape measure, whips it around, and he builds a brand-new hand cart for it that fits right into the truck compartment. On wheels. One guy can handle it on his own. No sweat.

JOAN   Sounds ingenious.

NICK   We didn't even know we needed it. Nobody asked him to do anything. He just thought of it and did it.

JOAN   He could have been an inventor.

NICK   Oh, he woulda been a great inventor. Everything this man built was made out of metal, and it was made right. We'd send him to the hardware store to buy something, and he'd say, "Nah, it was too flimsy." And he'd make it himself. And he made it to last. His bench—it's bolted to the floor. You can't move that thing. One guy transferred in to the company, he brought this weight-lifting rack and put it up in the workout room. All the guys used it. He gets transferred out, and he says, "I'm taking my equipment with me." Barney looks at Dave and says, "Oh no he's not." So Barney goes and welds it all together. You can use it, but you can't take it apart and get it out the door. That thing will be there forever. Nothin' that guy could do about it.

(He relishes it) He was mad.

(Pause)

Everybody else was on duty. But I wasn't sure about Barney. He wasn't on duty. But he never called in. The whole time I was getting all the other reports, part of me was thinking, Where's Barney?

JOAN   What happened?

NICK   *(He stands and looks into the distance)* The time

went by. And we remembered the videotape from the security camera at the firehouse. And we watch the tape. It's almost nine in the morning, and Barney pulls up in his van and gets out. Then he's there talking to Dave. And you see the street and the sidewalk . . . suddenly filling with papers . . . *(Slowly, watching it in his inner eye)* The companies go. Barney and Dave go. You see them both turn and walk away. Helmets . . . equipment . . . they walk away . . .

(The lights dim, then come up as two spots. JOAN *faces the audience on stage left.* NICK, *in uniformed funeral attire, stands and faces the audience formally, with the written eulogy in front of him)*

JOAN   When do we go back to normal? I asked someone that the other day: Will we go back to normal? He said, "Yes, we'll go back to normal. But normal will be different. This *is* the new normal."

The city is different. We lost our—jazz. We're muted. We lost—a lot.

NICK   *(He begins the oratory, in a simple, unpretentious, dignified way. He reads well and confidently, with affection. He's in control)* "I am Nick Flanagan of Ladder Company 60. I am here to honor the memory of our dear friend and brother Bernhardt Keppel.

I want to offer my most sincere condolences to his parents, Mr. and Mrs. Keppel, here with us today. *(He nods to the side)* I hope that these few words can give you some sense of how much we thought of Barney, and of the light he brought into our lives."

JOAN   Some days I can almost go without thinking about it. But to really pull that off, I'd have to avoid the newspaper, not watch TV news. Not do a lot of things. Not hear a siren, not smell smoke.

NICK   "What can I tell you about Barney? He lifted your heart. He had an unstoppable sense of humor. He was fun. He had a happy laugh. It rose out of him and took you along. For Barney, humor was as natural as breathing. But Barney also had an art, the metalworker's art. He recuperated things. There was nothing he loved more than fatigued metal."

JOAN   I get angry. How do you cut deals with God? Under these conditions?

NICK   "Barney was a genius with metal. He could weld it, bend it, bolt it, drill it—you name it. And then he brought in—creativity. He'd notice something around the firehouse that didn't work very well, something we just took for granted. And he'd think up a solution. Like the huge generator—the Hurst Tool—that's mounted on the rig for car accidents. One day Barney builds us a specially designed hand truck that fits right into the compartment. He's fixed something before we even defined the problem. That's the kind of guy he was."

JOAN   I know my terms. I realized it the other day getting on the subway. *(She changes to a defiant tone)* I want them back. I want them back. All of them. That's all I'll settle for. I want them back, just the way they were. I want them all back, together again. That's final.

NICK   "We depend on our tools. They're all important. When you go out on a call, sometimes you break through metal, sometimes wood. You need different tools. When you're answering an alarm, every tool counts."

JOAN   *(Desperate, methodical)* I'll tell you how it can work. I read about it in a book. Let's just play the tape backwards. Start with a shot of the rubble. The dust and steel rise and untwist, and form back up into buildings. The flames are sucked back into Tower Two, then Tower One. The planes fly backwards across the river, take a curve, and land backwards in Boston.

Everyone gets out of the plane and drives backwards home.

NICK   "But it's also how you use your tools. Barney set

up his own workshop at the firehouse, and it is a thing of beauty: a tool for everything, and every tool in its place. He built the workbench himself and bolted it to the floor. I can tell you, that workbench isn't going anywhere. If Barney built it, he built it well. Meticulous. Barney had a unique talent, and he used it for the betterment of the company. Here was a man who worked magic with his hands, respected his tools, and respected his job. The Department can't ask any more than that. Yet he brought so much more. He made us smile—and he still does, just thinking of him. He made us laugh. He made us feel good about who we were. About working with each other."

JOAN   The guys from the ladder truck run backwards. Barney's there. He's next to Dave. This time Jimmy's in front and Patrick's in back. They all get into the truck, back up. The orange traffic cone falls out on the street, and the truck backs into the station. Barney gets into his van and backs off home.

That's it. That's the deal.

But. I just . . . I just have nothing to bring to the table.

(She wilts)

NICK   "But trust Barney to leave us something more earthly, too. His careful hands built things to last. The tools he built for us are still in the firehouse. They're with us. They're anchored. They're welded. They're bolted. They're grounding us. We use them every day. And every time we touch them, we are grateful we could share his light."

(They look at each other across the stage. He is consoling, she is distraught. The lights go out)

Afterword

The firefighters came tentatively at first. Often, one man would come from a firehouse, and then a few performances later, others from the same firehouse would appear, frequently with their wives or girlfriends. I would see them watching the performance intently, clutching each other's hands in the dark. Often they would approach us afterward, in pairs or small groups, to talk. Sometimes they would exchange a look and say, "Now my wife knows what it's about." A handsome, weathered man came up to me after the play and said, "I'm a captain. That could have been any one of us." Firefighters would talk about their favorite lines from the play. One was Joan's: "Was I outside of it? I didn't want to be—not so far. This is my city, too." They welcomed evidence that outsiders wanted to stand by them. Another firefighter was glad that Nick called fire fighting "the best job in the world" and stuck to it.

"It still is," the young man told me firmly. "No doubt."

Early in December, we had contacted the Fire Department headquarters and told them about the play. We set aside blocks of seats for anyone connected with the firefighting community or the Port Authority Police, who had also lost an unthinkable proportion of their officers. Early on, I heard from the Fire Department's eulogy team. Its members were responsible for drafting eulogies for the 343 missing firefighters in the space of only a few months, for officials to deliver at services. It was unimaginable. The half-dozen members of the team came to the play, then invited me out to Brooklyn for lunch, along with some friends from the Fire Department press office, where they shared their stories with me. The team spent months interviewing hundreds of grieving survivors over the phone. The first thing they faced in the office each day were hundreds of personnel files corresponding to the lost men, propped up in an anonymous cardboard box.

At first, it was clear that no one who walked into the theater to see *The Guys* knew what to expect. I know that some people arrived with a sense of dread, fearing that they were facing ninety minutes of unrelieved gloom. The humor in the play would sneak up on them, the way it had with the actors, and there were split seconds when you could see them wondering whether it was okay to laugh. Many cried as well. I remember glancing at a woman sitting near me. Tears started to stream down her face as soon as the play began, yet a few minutes later she began to laugh softly. Afterward, the comment I heard most often from New Yorkers was "You put what I was feeling into words."

Many of the firefighters were fascinated by the reporting process, especially at the way they said the play captured "the lingo." They were surprised that I had never used a tape recorder—I listened hard, kept my eyes open, and took really fast notes.

But they also helped me catch mistakes. In the early weeks of the run, I had the captain refer to the "fire station."

"Hey, what's this 'fire station' stuff?" a firefighter asked me in December. "Maybe that's what they say out west or something. But here in the city, it's a 'firehouse.'" Who knew? But I checked around, and he was right, of course. My brother had been a volunteer fireman in a fire *station* in Stillwater,

Oklahoma. There were even fire stations as nearby as Schenectady. But in New York City, it's a fire*house*. I changed it (except for some passages spoken by Joan, who, after all, is from "out west").

Some reviewers seemed puzzled by *The Guys,* wondering whether it wasn't "journalism" more than "literature." They weren't sure whether to call it "traditional" or "experimental." I didn't write it with any preconceptions, only with two goals: to confront our city's devastation in a humane fashion and to help the theater company.

Some of the most intriguing comments were from psychiatrists, psychologists, and counselors who came to see the play. Some of them were working with the Fire Department's Counseling Services Unit. All of them were struggling with the professional pressure of trying to heal the damage of 9/11. Some called the play "therapeutic." After a number of conversations along this line, we reflected that both theater and psychology traced their vocabulary back to the Greeks: *drama* and *psyche* to start with, but also *catharsis, crisis,* and *therapy.* A play couldn't cure anyone. But it could bring people together in a dedicated space and allow them to experience emotion together. From my limited knowledge of the ancient Greeks and their theater, this wasn't so far from their intent.

The Flea Theater scheduled the play to run from December 4 to December 18, 2001, with Sigourney Weaver and Bill Murray in the two roles. I went to every one of these performances, and usually sat quietly in the back. Often there was an emotional charge that took us all aback, and the actors would leave the theater looking drained. Part of me feared that it was putting too much of a strain on them to perform the play every night, and I felt that the least I could do was be present.

Some nights I listened to the play as a writer and made small changes to the script the following day. Sometimes I listened as a member of the audience and felt the strange intensity that was connecting a roomful of strangers. Sometimes I heard the play directly, seeing each man described in it and reliving the loss.

The play pretty much sold out before it opened. By the end of December, it was obvious that the run would be extended, and the cast began to go into rotation. The script was "set." My teaching semester began, and I went to the theater much less often, usually when I knew friends were going or when someone I'd met from a firehouse was attending and might want to talk about it afterward.

The reactions in December were very raw—barely three months had passed since the attack, and New Yorkers' emotions were still close to the surface. Some people came to the play and visibly mourned those they'd lost. Others who, like Joan, had not lost anyone close to them, told us the play allowed them to reconnect with emotions that had been pushed away or submerged too quickly.

As the months wore on, *The Guys* changed from a reflection of the present into a memory play of the recent past. After the January run, new actors came to the production. Bill Irwin, Susan Sarandon, Tim Robbins, and Swoozie Kurtz inherited the roles in turn, each bringing his or her new insights to the play. Jim Simpson chose two members of the Flea's resident company, Tim Cummings and Irene Walsh, as understudies. Each brought a special connection to the play. Tim Cummings is the son of a retired firefighter, and Irene's mother had actually worked as a welder. Their work was too good to waste, and we soon had them giving pro bono performances around town to audiences who wouldn't have been able to see the play otherwise.

Without a doubt, the most moving encounters I had after the performances were with survivors of those lost on September 11. They were the heart of the experience for me, and I will never forget them.

To comprehend the magnitude of what happened to the firehouses of New York on September 11, it helps to understand some things about the firehouses themselves. The Fire Department lists 203 engine companies and 143 ladder companies, scattered across the five boroughs of New York. There are also battalion units, rescue companies (which specialize in helping firefighters in perilous operations), squads (specialized engine companies that assist with rescue operations), and the Haz-Mat company, a highly trained unit that disposes of explosives, toxic chemicals, medical waste, and other hazardous materials. Combined, these forces comprise about 8,600 firefighters, 530 captains, and 1,430 lieutenants. The department also includes 2,650 emergency medical technicians and paramedics, 200 fire marshals, and 1,700 administrative and support staff. There are nearly 400 chiefs of various ranks. A few of the fire-fighting companies trace their roots back to the mid-1700s, and some of them have occupied the same firehouses for a hundred years.

The Fire Department's headquarters are located in a streamlined, modern office building in a new Brooklyn development called Metro Tech. Despite its conventional exterior, the Fire Department does not function like any other city agency known to man. There are volumes of regulations, unspoken codes of honor, and fierce traditions. At the same time, each firehouse has its own character, and many of them pride themselves on a certain irreverence toward higher authority. The firehouses are more like an alliance of microstates than a sharply defined hierarchy.

Most New York City firehouses combine engine and ladder companies, whose teams are fairly separate and work in shifts. Each company has about twenty to twenty-five personnel, who rotate through "tours" that usually consist of five men and an officer. There is a (mosty friendly) rivalry between engine and ladder. Ladder men say that engine men are shorter—traditionally, to help keep them below the level of the smoke when they "put wet stuff on the red stuff." Even so, they often have to hit the floor and "suck linoleum." The ladder men are allegedly taller and work like a benevolent combination of burglar and wrecking crew. Their forcible-entry team enters locked buildings, locating trapped occupants and poking into the innards of walls and ceilings with hooks and Halligans to hunt down any embers that could reignite. (The Halligan tool is a device developed in New York more than fifty years ago by first deputy fire commissioner Hugh Halligan. Adopted by emergency teams all over the country, it looks like a medieval instrument of torture, with wicked-looking metal implements perfectly balanced on either end of a long stick.)

I've heard ladder men call engine men "the little guys with the hoses" and engine men insinuate that ladder men are not quite their equals in intelligence. But the truth of the matter is that firefighters do switch from one to the other, and many friendships exist across engine/ladder lines.

Among firefighters, the emphasis is on teamwork over regimentation. Professionalism—meaning competence, dependability, and effort—is prized above all. Just behind that come the qualities of humor, loyalty, and generosity. Not every fire-fighter has all of these qualities, but they keep pretty close tabs on who has which.

These traits are apparent in daily life at many firehouses. There is a lively interest in the meals—which, by the way, can be questionable, but can also be excellent. (Nick Flanagan's remark about "valiant attempts and dismal failures" should be taken as the firehouse habit to mix friendly put-downs with self-deprecation.)

Firefighters keep a close eye on who lends a hand without being asked and who dodges a job, and judge one another ac-cordingly. These practices are carried into their personal lives as well. One firefighter told me how he and his wife bought a "fixer-upper" on Long Island and needed help putting on a new roof. "I wrote on the board in the kitchen that if a cou-ple of guys showed up, I'd give them free beer," he said. On the appointed day, a dozen firefighters arrived and did a six-day job in two, at no cost (other than a few cases of beer). It's hard to imagine that happening at many workplaces.

And if firefighters look out for one another's homesteads on an informal basis, they assume a sacred oath to look after one another's families. After September 11, this promise took on awe-inspiring dimensions.

Some firehouses have the reputation of being fractious, but when a firehouse is close-knit, the firefighters spend a lot of time together off duty as well as on the job (even after living with one another for twenty-four-hour shifts!). The walls of these firehouses are covered with snapshots of family picnics, shared vacations ranging from skiing to scuba diving, and community projects on days off, quite often involving little kids. Many firefighters seem to have a special affinity for chil-dren, which may be partly protective and partly a matter of shared values. "Some kids want to grow up to be firefighters," goes the saying, "but you can't do both."

The schedule of the job—often a twenty-four-hour shift on duty, followed by two days off—encourages a varied life. Some firefighters have thriving businesses on the side, often drawing on their mechanical skills in fields like construction or auto repair. Many of them are active fathers, taking on the lion's share of child care while their wives are at the office. Many others use their time off to immerse themselves in the arts. Get a bunch of firefighters into a room and you might find actors, singers, rock musicians, stage designers, sculptors, and, yes, ballroom dancers, to say nothing of world travelers and athletes practicing every imaginable sport. They tend to be serious about their avocations, and good at them more often than not. There are also fugitives from more sedate professions: lawyers, stockbrokers, and accountants.

The nature of the job varies from neighborhood to neighborhood. You don't have to spend much time around firefighters to learn that poor people have both the most fires and the worst fires, so the poor neighborhoods are the ones with the busiest firehouses. Most firefighters would rather work in a busy firehouse (within reason) than a slow one. That's where they feel they make the biggest difference; that's where their skills are honed and tested. The South Bronx and Brooklyn's Bedford-Stuyvesant (known as Bed-Stuy) are two neighborhoods of choice.

Somewhere in the unwritten stories of New York firefighters, you could trace the hidden history of the city. Fire companies have existed in New York since the 1600s, and by the nineteenth century they had initiated firefighting techniques that continue to develop to this day. They were badly needed. Ever-growing waves of immigrants were thrown into hastily erected blocks of wooden housing and sweatshops, many of them notorious firetraps. The early firefighters were known to relish a hearty brawl from time to time, but they also performed many daring rescues. As the number of fire companies grew, they incorporated droves of the new Irish-Americans. These were among the earliest volunteers in the Union army, including the colorful Zouaves. A few firefighters joined in the bloody draft riots of 1863, but many more of them struggled to put the fires out. In 1865, city officials converted the fire companies (in those days, "engine," "hose," and "hook and ladder") from a volunteer force to a professional fire department.

If you want to understand why there are still so many Irish firefighters, all you need to do is go to an Irish Catholic memorial service in one of the outer boroughs. "He wanted to be a firefighter since he was five." "His father and three uncles were in the Fire Department." "All of his best friends became firefighters." "From the time he was in grade school, the firefighters in the neighborhood picked him out as a good prospect." Perhaps in the early days, a career in firefighting merely represented a decent paying job for men who faced discrimination in other fields and had little access to formal education. But generations of firefighters made it something else, something incalculably rare: a job they loved.

Now it's common for applicants to pass the test and mark three or four years working at something else, waiting for an opening before they can join. Firefighter fathers roll their eyes at the mention of sons who pull down good money on Wall Street, only to drop it the minute they can join the Department at a fraction of the pay. But make no mistake—the firefighter fathers are proud of their sons' choice.

If you look at any given roster of New York City firefighters, you'll still see a preponderance of Irish names. Many others are Italian. Then there are smatterings of Hispanic, German, Eastern European, Norwegian, and African-American (including Afro-Caribbean). They are overwhelmingly men—due, I'm told, both to the culture and to a physical examination that stresses upper-body strength that few women develop (and is also an insurmountable challenge for many men). The first women were admitted to the Department in 1982, following a change in the physical examination. Some of them have held their own professionally and risen through the ranks. But the path has not been easy, and they've advised the current generation of female firefighters following in their footsteps that they will need to hold on to every ounce of their determination.

I was surprised at what a strongly marked generational sense there was among firefighters. I had expected the ties of ethnicity and esprit de corps to dominate the culture, but to some extent firefighters (like the rest of us, I suppose) are products of their time. In the 1970s, when New York faced bankruptcy, the Fire Department cut costs through attrition. Retiring firefighters weren't replaced, and the ranks were drastically depleted. When the economy began to recover in the 1980s, unusually large classes of recruits were brought in, and, logically enough, many of them were children of the sixties. I don't know why, but it still throws me to meet a fifty-something fire captain, with his officer's air of authority and military bearing, who tells me he spends his weekends playing electric guitar.

Many officers in the firehouses, now in their late forties and fifties, are Vietnam veterans who returned to America bruised by the war, only to be greeted with indifference or, worse, disdain for their service. No matter what their politics, veterans among the firefighters have told me that the transition from the military to the Fire Department made sense. One retired fire chief explained to me that both ways of life offered the camaraderie and physical challenges of military culture. "But when you're a firefighter," he said, "you're saving people's lives instead of taking them."

———

For weeks after 9/11, I struggled to make sense of it through the information on offer: images of chaos and numbers. On the first day, some news media reported that there were as many as 15,000 dead in the World Trade Center. That number fell steadily, and by early 2002 it finally started to settle at 2,830. One day, reading the paper, it hit me that roughly 12 percent—one in eight—of the people who died in the World Trade Center were firefighters. The reason was simple: While everyone else was struggling to get out, they were still going in. Unknown numbers of civilians were saved by their actions.

The Fire Department's casualties on September 11 were not evenly distributed across the city. In recent years, an average of two or three firefighters have been killed in action over a given year. In the blessed years 1988, 1990, and 1997, no one died in the line of duty. As of August 2001, firefighters were still shaken by the Father's Day fire in Queens a few months earlier that killed three of their number. In the lobby of the Department's headquarters at Metro Tech, there is a large plaque on the wall with the names of the 778 firefighters killed on duty since the founding of the department in 1865—until September 11. As of the beginning of September, the wall was filled up to the last twenty spots. I was told that first deputy commissioner William Feehan used to walk by and say he hoped he would reach retirement before those spots were filled up. Feehan was killed on September 11 with other high-ranking fire officials in the command bunker.

The vast majority of firefighters killed on September 11 were from Manhattan and Brooklyn firehouses.

———

Consider this:

There are 143 ladder companies in New York City, 32 of which (just over one fifth) are in Manhattan. Twenty-eight of the New York City ladder companies lost at least one man, and almost two thirds of those companies were in Manhattan. Fifteen companies lost five men or more, the equivalent of an entire tour. Eleven of the 15 were in Manhattan, south of Eighty-sixth Street, in a concentration of only a few square miles.

The picture is similar for the engine companies: There are 203 engine companies in New York City, 41 of them in Manhattan. Thirty-two engine companies lost someone, 17 of them in Manhattan. Eleven lost four or more men—7 of them in Manhattan.

These terrible concentrations of casualties were repeated—in equally devastating fashion—in the Special Operations Command, or SOC, units. All five Rescue companies, each located in a different borough, lost an entire tour. Five of the seven squads lost a full tour. The Haz-Mat company lost a battalion chief, a lieutenant, and six men: an entire crew. Twenty-three staff and battalion chiefs were lost, decimating a generation of leadership.

Much of the pattern was determined by blind geography. Firehouses in Manhattan and Brooklyn got the calls first, and arrived within the first hour after the attack. A little later, firefighters from more remote firehouses and others who were off duty tried to get to the site, but were stranded on highways and intersections—snarls in logistics that saved their lives.

It is devastating to lose even one friend and colleague. Fire-fighters who emerged from September 11 with their companies intact still lost friends from previous assignments or classmates from the probie academy. No one in the Fire Department was unscathed. Older firefighters, who might have lost one or two acquaintances over a twenty-year career, now spoke of losing fifty or sixty friends, then losing count, then trying not to count anymore.

It seemed to me that the companies that had suffered immense casualties had entered into another dimension of loss. In these small, close-knit workplaces, your workmates greased the wheels of daily life, but they also defended your life when you took on a fire. Suddenly the community had a large hole blown into it. Not only were you likely to have lost a close friend, but there was nothing in your daily experience that resembled the past. It reminded me of villages I'd read of in Eastern Europe after World War II. Suddenly, half of the population was gone. There could be no routine, and every failed function was a reminder of catastrophe.

The bureaucratic machinery strained to the breaking point. How could any institution deal with so many widows, so many memorial services, so many death benefits, so many emotions that had nowhere to go? A fire captain's daily job continued to be the oversight of a company that responded to emergencies and put out fires. But in many firehouses there was now layer upon layer of additional duties, agonizing in their nature. Each affected firehouse assigned a team of men to make regular visits to bereaved family members, to help them face the many burdens of sudden death.

The remaining men struggled with guilt: Why are they

dead and we're not? Anger: Who did this to us and how can we strike back? Officers had to keep their men calm and engaged, to watch out for danger signs. The fallen men had to be replaced—so the city wouldn't burn down. Three new classes of probies was rushed through the academy and assigned to the firehouses. Firefighters were moved down from firehouses in distant parts of the city. Ten and ten, the firehouse directly across the street from Ground Zero, had lost four men and its building was knocked out of commission, so its surviving men were split up and temporarily assigned to other firehouses. The new men, the displaced, and the fill-ins found their new coworkers carrying out their routines in dazed silence, still in a state of shock, the ghosts of the men they replaced very much at hand.

Overnight, firehouses underwent a physical conversion as well. Usually, the entryway of a firehouse gives the impression of a good-natured garage: You're surrounded by oversize vehicles and tools; the sharp smell of diesel and lubricant hangs in the air. Now the afflicted houses turned into shrines. Photos of the fallen were placed at the door, and gardens of artifacts sprang up beneath: notes, candles, flowers, stuffed animals, shoulder patches from firefighters visiting from great distances. Inside, the firehouses were wallpapered with notes, most of them from children. Many included drawings of planes crashing into the towers, with firefighters on ladders that reached magically to the top. Sometimes the messages were simple expressions of gratitude or patriotism. Sometimes they were more disconcerting. "Dear Firemen, Thank you for saving everyone in the World Trade Center. I'm glad none of you were hurt."

The firehouses in many neighborhoods became places where civilians came to seek comfort. Friendships were forged.

But sometimes the firefighters just longed to get back to a routine and put out a couple of good fires. The firefighters sensed that they had been through a cataclysm, but nothing had ever prepared them—or anyone—to confront it. Some firehouses went quiet, with tacit understanding of the suffering that was going on in their midst, but no way to talk about it. "My Irish mother called me up after it happened," one firefighter told me. "She said, 'Son, remember how our kind handle such things—bury it! If you don't talk about it, it will go away.' "

"Burying it" didn't always work. Some men went through a repertory of classic symptoms: explosive anger, sleeplessness, numbness. Counselors offered their services. Many firefighters resisted—counseling, in their minds, was for drunks and loonies. Gradually they started to come around, to accept help. It was hard. These were people who defined themselves as the rescuers. And everyone knew that, at best, help could take the edge off, keep them safe until enough time had passed. Help couldn't fix everything that was wrong.

The memorial services began the first week, and it seemed they'd never end. A full Fire Department service entails a ceremony that has evolved over generations: a corps of bagpipers who play the same four traditional airs at every service; row upon row of blue-uniformed personnel, firefighters in dark blue hats, officers in white ones; an official helicopter flyover at the end, with Department buglers playing taps. It is a service whose depth and intensity should limit its use to rare intervals. Yet over the fall and much of the winter, it was presented several times a week, sometimes with multiple services taking place simultaneously in different boroughs or suburbs. The band of bagpipers had to be divided up, and when they started to weary, former members had to be summoned out of retirement. Every family that wanted a service received one—that was the pledge. The faces of the families were always fresh with grief, but the faces of the bagpipers wore down over the months like weathered rock. Their music was always perfect, their gait precise. The odds dictated that sooner or later, every bagpiper played at a service for someone he knew—who knows how many? But the bagpipes are demanding. They want a focused mind and a solid embouchure. It doesn't do to think too much.

There were grim new logistics to plan. The Catholic Church requires that for full funeral rites, there must be remains. In December, *Fireworks,* the Fire Department newsletter, printed an advisory from a Department chaplain, describing a meeting that was held September 13:

> Two of the questions posed were, "How do we celebrate 343 funerals?" and "How is it possible to give each one of our fallen Firefighters the honor and respect that each has earned?" Little did we know that many of these celebrations would be Memorial Masses or Memorial Services [a mass or service without a body].

He proceeded to give officers advice for informing families of the recovery of fragments, sometimes over stages, since this was the way it was starting to go.

As the memorial services continued in the outer boroughs, teams of firefighters and police searched for remains. It wasn't always clear that city officials wanted the teams to be searching the site, but it was always clear that the teams intended to be there.

They started out as volunteers and, for the most part, continued on that basis. Usually, there were three teams of a dozen men. They worked twelve-hour shifts, then had two days off, alternating daytime and nighttime duty for a month. Almost everyone digging at the site was a member of the uniformed services, but I was told that sometimes widows and other survivors joined in. A cluster of retired fire officials came every day, many of them because they had lost their sons and hoped to help find them. In late winter a friend who was working at the site asked me if I'd like to come along. I wanted to know what they were going through. We went downtown and suited up in Carhartts, the regulation baggy brown overalls, quilted jacket, and hard hat. We wore thick work gloves and carried cumbersome respirators with an elaborate system of straps to fasten them on our heads.

I had seen the site from a viewing platform, but it was nothing like being inside. From the outside it looked like a moderate-size construction site, but from below, it was like being at the bottom of a vast canyon, dampened by foul rivers and scraped raw by machines. The rubble wasn't smoldering anymore, but sometimes the earth-moving tools would heat lodes of buried metal until steam rose up from the mound. In the beginning, people digging out the site had called it the Pile, and then the Pit, as if they could hurl anger at the attack by insulting the place where it happened. But over time they came to feel that these words lacked respect. By the time I got there, it was just the Site.

New Yorkers often remark how strangely beautiful the weather was for most of the fall and winter of 2001–2002— winter never really came—and the day I visited was no exception. The sun shone yellow-white. I looked at the array of equipment that was assembled for the job: bulldozers, excavators, grapplers, backhoes, everything my son adored when he was two. A dozen of us worked on our team, and several other teams toiled nearby. We stood with clawed rakes on a small, flat upper surface, in the shadow of the offices *The Wall Street Journal* had occupied until it was blown out of them. The grappler scooped out bucketfuls of earth and debris and dumped it in front of us. A spreader arrayed it across the ground and we went to work, combing the piles for anything human.

My friend had been working all month. The hardest part, he said, was going for days without finding any remains. But the previous week they had found part of a bone. This was good. With DNA identification, it meant that someone would have something to bury.

It was backbreaking work. The rake would catch its teeth in twisted metal rods and have to be pulled hard or shaken loose. We shifted slabs of metal and rock to make sure we didn't miss anything underneath. We scrutinized scraps, hopeful and fearful at the same time. Most loads were futile. The small white chip was porcelain, not bone. The yellowish fragment was only paper. It became clear that the only thing worse than finding something was not finding something. In the meantime, the debris yielded clues of a vanished civilization: bundles of T-shirts, still folded, reading WWW.THEBEAST.COM; telephone books and blue cloth-covered arms of couches; I.D. cards and calling cards and Metrocards for the subway. Occasionally, there would be a shoe or a shirt, but these were of no interest. "You can't bury a shirt," one of the men said, and shrugged. We went through the load as carefully as we could. Then it was scooped up and shipped off to the landfill, and another bucketful arrived.

A little later, a firefighter working the Site told me that his team had found a body a few days earlier, including an identifying Claddagh ring. They met the widow the next day and received her thanks. "Finding him for her was one of the best things I've ever done," he said quietly.

Work at the Site was finished in the late spring of 2002.

The Fire Department's "Running Total of Recoveries" reported that as of March 29, 2002, more than six months after the attack, 285 whole bodies had been found and 18,232 partial human remains. Only 878 of the 2,830 victims had been identified, including 170 of the 343 firefighters. The unidentified remains were taken away for DNA testing, which was expected to take several years to complete.

Periodically, I hear people comment that "it's time to move on," that "the firefighters need to understand that." All I can think of is what the fire captain told me late in the fall: "For us, every day in the firehouse is September 12." And it will be, for some time to come.

I don't think that terms like *move on* and *closure* offer us much. The very fact we use them suggests we're forcing the issue. Instead, the aftermath of the attack unfolds in chapters over time, and we have no choice but to move through them as they come. The question is, What will we learn from this experience? One place to start could be the simple but demanding lesson of the firehouse: Honor belongs to those who "use their talent for the betterment of the company."

Suggested Reading

The Guys is, first and foremost, an homage to New York's firefighters. Those who would like to learn more about them could start with Dennis Smith's *Report from Engine Co. 82* (Warner Books, 1999). Smith was a firefighter in the South Bronx in the 1970s, at a time when the area was ravaged by arson. This book gives a vivid sense of life inside the firehouse and the understated but powerful bonds of friendship among the men.

Smith has revisited the subject of fire fighting a number of times. *Firefighters: Their Lives in Their Own Words* is based on interviews with firefighters across the United States. Smith's latest work, *Report from Ground Zero,* was published by Viking in January 2002. It combines narrative writing with oral history to recount the experiences of members of the New York Fire Department on September 11.

An underlying theme in *The Guys* is the nature of trauma. Certain professional cultures—fire fighting and journalism among them—have a long-standing tradition of "toughing it out." There is increasing recognition that the failure to deal with trauma in the long term can have devastating consequences for individuals and their families. One book that addresses these issues in a broad fashion is *Trauma and Recovery* (Basic Books, 1997), by Judith Herman, M.D. Herman, a professor of psychiatry at Harvard Medical School, writes clearly and compassionately. Although her point of departure is trauma arising from domestic violence and sexual abuse, her later chapters, on "Terror," "Safety," and "Reconnection," are extremely applicable to the aftermath of 9/11.

There is growing interest in the relationship between the news media, violence, and trauma. *Covering Violence: A Guide to Ethical Reporting About Victims and Trauma,* by William Coté and Roger Simpson (Columbia University Press, 2000), is a major contribution to the field. It includes perspectives on the ways in which journalists experience secondary trauma and how it can affect their work. Simpson, a former reporter, is the director of the Dart Center for Journalism and Trauma at the University of Washington, which has an excellent website, with additional resources.

Among the many books about bereavement, one stands out in my mind: *Another Path,* by Gladys Taber (Lippincott, 1963). It is a gentle chronicle of Taber's struggle to readjust to a new life—"the new normal"—after the death of her dearest friend, through meditations on the restorative powers of nature. The book is thoughtful but indirect, and even the rhythms of the prose are soothing. Although Taber was a bestselling author in the 1950s and 1960s, the book is now out of print. There are hopes it will be reissued soon.

In several passages of *The Guys,* Joan relates her experiences in the dirty wars of Latin America to the shock of September 11. Those wars, in many ways a final chapter of the Cold War, played out in many countries, including Chile, Argentina, El Salvador, Guatemala, and Nicaragua. There are a number of good books that deal with each country and region's particular history. But one of the most moving personal accounts of the period is *What Prize Awaits Us,* by Bernice Kita (Orbis Books, 1988). Kita is a Maryknoll Sister and worked for twenty-four years among the indigenous peoples of Guatemala, first in their highland villages and later in refugee camps across the Mexican border. In her book, she describes what it was like to witness attacks on her village first-hand—helpless to stop the violence but determined to accompany her parishioners through their ordeal. It is a beautiful portrait of how a community, and an extraordinary individual, wrestle with despair by drawing on faith.

Finally, three novels touch on various themes in the play. For a trenchant portrayal of the effects of "shell shock" on a company of World War II veterans, see James Jones's *Whistle,* the perceptive and sometimes startlingly frank third volume of his war trilogy. For a knowing portrait of Irish-American life in New York, look for Jimmy Breslin's book *Table Money.* And on the theme of political violence in Latin America, I recommend Isabel Allende's *House of the Spirits.* Many of its perspectives on Chile apply to the recent history of Argentina as well.

Acknowledgments

First and above all, I would like to thank Nick Flanagan for his friendship and his trust. Anything of worth within these pages is due to him and his community. I would also like to express my appreciation to his fellow captain, their chief, and the troops of the firehouse, who shared some samples of their cuisine and many cups of firehouse coffee (which was pretty good), a couple of beers (outside the firehouse), a large chunk of chocolate rabbit, and many acts of kindness along the way.

There are many others from the New York Fire Department, and from their families, who have given unstintingly of their time, their knowledge, and their friendship. They include Richard Fanning and his wife, Anita; Dennis Stanford and his daughters, Kaitlin and Amy; Dag Dorf and his wife, Patty; John McConnachie, his father, and his brother, Malcolm; Kevin Rice, Mike Kennedy, Jimmie Hanlin, Gerard Allas, and others. I thank the many firefighters and their families and friends who came to the play and took the time to talk afterward. I am also very grateful to the extended Barry and Olsen families and to Chris Colligan for the time and reflections they have shared with me. They are examples of courage and generosity in the midst of grief.

I thank Jim Simpson for his willingness to take risks and for his uncorrupted artistic vision. Sigourney Weaver and Bill Murray leapt into the unknown with this project and helped to shape it. Each subsequent cast member has brought something of value to it. I thank the members of the Bats Theater Company for their hospitality and inspiration. Tigran Eldred was another friend of the play from the beginning.

At Random House, I thank Kate Medina for her boldness and her assistant Jessica Kirshner for her attention, in commissioning this book and seeing it through.

I would also like to express my appreciation for a remarkable collection of people at ICM, who came upon a small play and helped it grow without compromising its spirit. They include Sam Cohn, Sarah Jane Leigh, Heather Schroeder, Bart Walker, David Schmerler, and their adept assistants.

At the Columbia Graduate School of Journalism, I would like to thank Tom Goldstein, for his combination of an intensely local and a resolutely global vision. Arlene Morgan has been a friend and mentor, and has understood from the beginning what this was all about. The RW1 faculty has taught me to look at my city with fresh eyes. My students, both past and present, have taught me a lot about the world and have informed many aspects of this play, as have my colleagues in Buenos Aires and Barcelona. Hiro and Michelle Tanaka, Leon Huang, and los Compadritos Clarinistas de BB.AA. inspired the tango.

Gerald Martone, Jack Saul, and Stefan Quentzel have helped me think about the nature of trauma, one of the themes of this play. Their work matters, and I hope to continue to learn from them. One passage of the play, "The Science of Pain," was adapted from the book *Listening to Prozac,* by Peter D. Kramer. The penultimate image of the play was inspired by a passage from *Slaughterhouse Five,* by Kurt Vonnegut.

I thank two men who taught me about writing, Charles Chessmore and Dick Humphries. Three communities have lent me help and cheer in many ways: Trinity School, St. Iggie's of Antioch, and the Maryknoll Sisters.

Finally, I would like to thank my sister, Jennifer, my brother-in-law, Burk Bilger, and Hans, Ruby, and Evangeline for their part in this story and for being their own good selves. My brother, Dr. Daniel Nelson, a gifted healer, has been a support and a partner over the years in responding first to the inhumanities of El Salvador, then Oklahoma City, then 9/11. I have drawn endlessly on his strength, intelligence, and compassion. My husband, George Black, and my children, David and Julia, have helped me make this unexpected journey. I cherish them.

This book was set in Sabon, a typeface designed by the well-known German typographer Jan Tschichold (1902–74). Sabon's design is based upon the original letter forms of Claude Garamond and was created specifically to be used for three sources: foundry type for hand composition, Linotype, and Monotype. Tschichold named his typeface for the famous Frankfurt typefounder Jacques Sabon, who died in 1580.